We Can Do It!

GROWING PLANTS

By Lois Fortuna

Gareth Stevens
PUBLISHING

Please visit our website, www.garethstevens.com. For a free color catalog of all our high-quality books, call toll free 1-800-542-2595 or fax 1-877-542-2596.

Cataloging-in-Publication Data

Fortuna, Lois.
Growing plants / by Lois Fortuna.
p. cm. — (We can do it!)
Includes index.
ISBN 978-1-4824-3803-1 (pbk.)
ISBN 978-1-4824-3804-8 (6-pack)
ISBN 978-1-4824-3805-5 (library binding)
1. Growth (Plants) — Juvenile literature. 2. Plants — Juvenile literature. 3. Gardening — Juvenile literature. I. Fortuna, Lois. II. Title.
QK731.F67 2016
630—d23

First Edition

Published in 2016 by
Gareth Stevens Publishing
111 East 14th Street, Suite 349
New York, NY 10003

Editor: Ryan Nagelhout
Designer: Laura Bowen

Photo credits: Cover, pp. 1, 5, 9 matka_Wariatka/Shutterstock.com; pp. 7, 24 (seeds) Mona Makela/Shutterstock.com; p. 11 PeopleImages.com/Digital Vision/Getty Images; pp. 13, 24 (vegetables) Dan Kosmayer/Shutterstock.com; p. 15 Dorling Kindersley/Getty Images; p. 17 Stocksnapper/Shutterstock.com; p. 19 stuart.ford/Shutterstock.com; p. 21 Margit Litschel/Getty Images; p. 23 mexrix/Shutterstock.com.

Printed in the United States of America

CPSIA compliance information: Batch #CW16GS: For further information contact Gareth Stevens, New York, New York at 1-800-542-2595.

Contents

Growing plants is easy!

Most plants come from seeds.

I like to grow flowers.

My dad has a garden.

He grows plants we eat!
These are called vegetables.

I dig in the ground.

Seeds go in the hole.

We cover the seeds.

Next, we water the ground.

Soon the plants
start to grow!

Words to Know

seeds

vegetables

Index